Cram101 Textbook Outlines to accompany:

Industrial Organizational Psychology: Research and Practice

Spector, 3rd Edition

An Academic Internet Publishers (AIPI) publication (c) 2007.

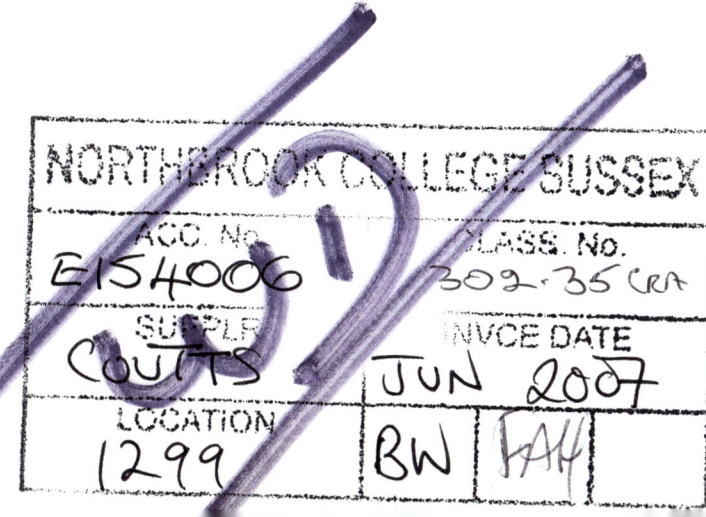

You have a discounted membership at www.Cram101.com with this book.

Get all of the practice tests for the chapters of this textbook, and access in-depth reference material for writing essays and papers. Here is an example from a Cram101 Biology text:

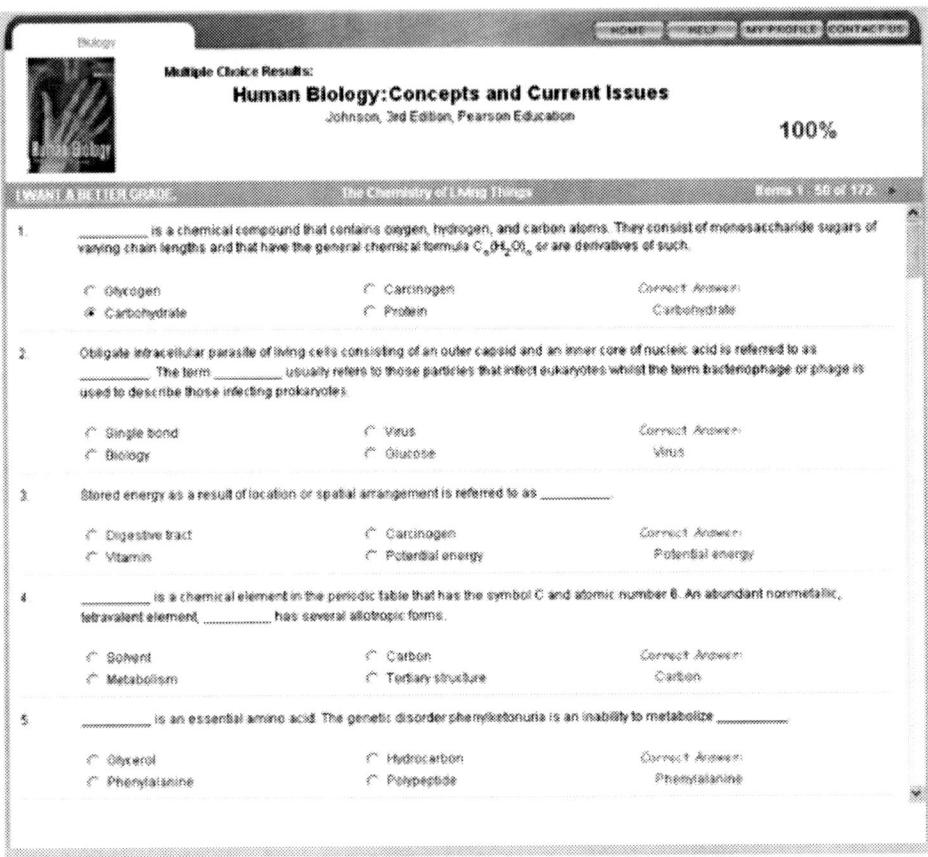

When you need problem solving help with math, stats, and other disciplines, www.Cram101.com will walk through the formulas and solutions step by step.

With Cram101.com online, you also have access to extensive reference material.

You will nail those essays and papers. Here is an example from a Cram101 Biology text:

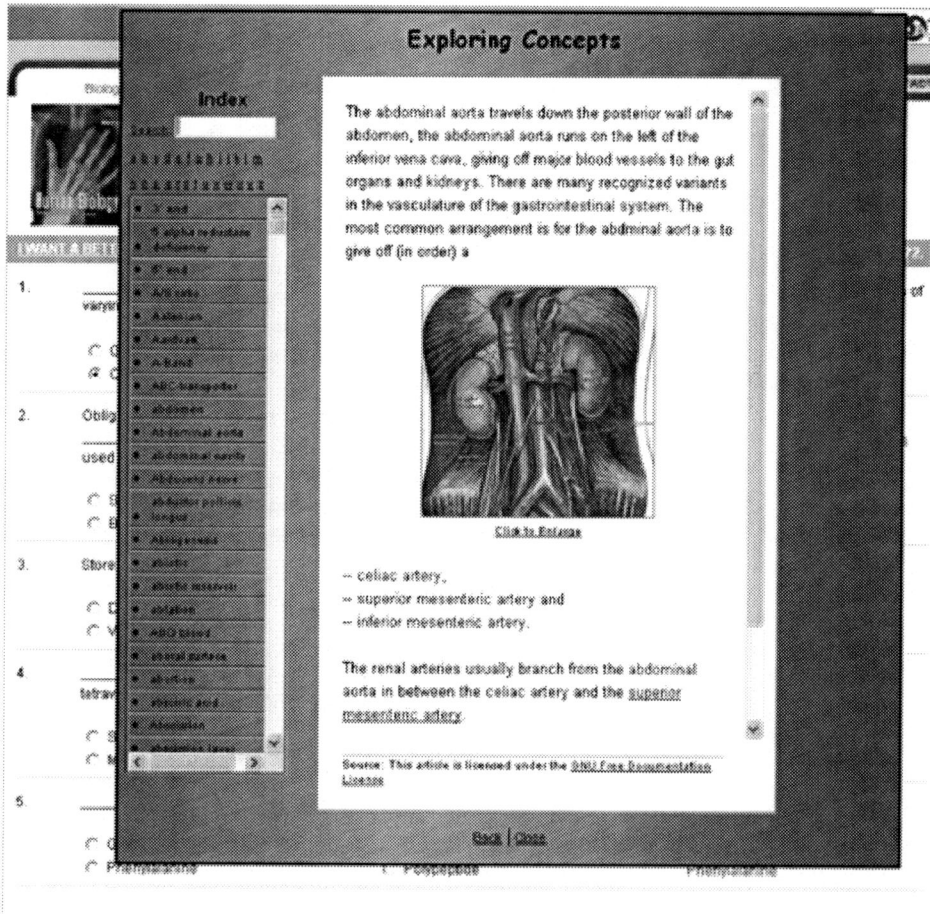

Visit **www.Cram101.com**, click Sign Up at the top of the screen, and enter DK73DW in the promo code box on the registration screen. Access to www.Cram101.com is normally $9.95, but because you have purchased this book, your access fee is only $4.95. Sign up and stop highlighting textbooks forever.

Learning System

Cram101 Textbook Outlines is a learning system. The notes in this book are the highlights of your textbook, you will never have to highlight a book again.

How to use this book. Take this book to class, it is your notebook for the lecture. The notes and highlights on the left hand side of the pages follow the outline and order of the textbook. All you have to do is follow along while your intructor presents the lecture. Circle the items emphasized in class and add other important information on the right side. With Cram101 Textbook Outlines you'll spend less time writing and more time listening. Learning becomes more efficient.

Cram101.com Online

Increase your studying efficiency by using Cram101.com's practice tests and online reference material. It is the perfect complement to Cram101 Textbook Outlines. Use self-teaching matching tests or simulate in-class testing with comprehensive multiple choice tests, or simply use Cram's true and false tests for quick review. Cram101.com even allows you to enter your in-class notes for an integrated studying format combining the textbook notes with your class notes.

Visit **www.Cram101.com**, click Sign Up at the top of the screen, and enter **DK73DW364** in the promo code box on the registration screen. Access to www.Cram101.com is normally $9.95, but because you have purchased this book, your access fee is only $4.95. Sign up and stop highlighting textbooks forever.

Industrial Organizational Psychology: Research and Practice
Spector, 3rd

CONTENTS

Feedback	Feedback refers to information returned to a person about the effects a response has had.
Psychological test	Psychological test refers to a standardized measure of a sample of a person's behavior.
Motivation	In psychology, motivation is the driving force (desire) behind all actions of an organism.
Theories	Theories are logically self-consistent models or frameworks describing the behavior of a certain natural or social phenomenon. They are broad explanations and predictions concerning phenomena of interest.
Social psychology	Social psychology is the study of the nature and causes of human social behavior, with an emphasis on how people think towards each other and how they relate to each other.
Research method	The scope of the research method is to produce some new knowledge. This, in principle, can take three main forms: Exploratory research; Constructive research; and Empirical research.
Cognition	The intellectual processes through which information is obtained, transformed, stored, retrieved, and otherwise used is cognition.
Emotion	An emotion is a mental states that arise spontaneously, rather than through conscious effort. They are often accompanied by physiological changes.
Clinical psychology	Clinical psychology is involved in the diagnosis, assessment, and treatment of patients with mental or behavioral disorders, and conducts research in these various areas.
Clinical psychologist	A psychologist, usually with a Ph.D, whose training is in the diagnosis, treatment, or research of psychological and behavioral disorders is a clinical psychologist.
Psychological disorder	Mental processes and/or behavior patterns that cause emotional distress and/or substantial impairment in functioning is a psychological disorder.
Industrial/organizational psychology	Industrial/organizational psychology is an applied branch of psychology concerned with behavior of individuals and groups in organizations.
Alcoholism	A disorder that involves long-term, repeated, uncontrolled, compulsive, and excessive use of alcoholic beverages and that impairs the drinker's health and work and social relationships is called alcoholism.
Attitude	An enduring mental representation of a person, place, or thing that evokes an emotional response and related behavior is called attitude.
Industrial and organizational psychology	Industrial and organizational psychology is the study of the behavior of people in the workplace. Industrial and organizational psychology attempts to apply psychological results and methods to aid workers and organizations.
Survey	A method of scientific investigation in which a large sample of people answer questions about their attitudes or behavior is referred to as a survey.
Time and motion study	A time and motion study is an analysis of task performance involving the observation and timing of individuals' motions. The purpose is to determine ways to eliminate or modify motions to make performance more efficient.
Human factors	Human factors refers to the study of the interaction of people and machines. It is a technology that applies knowledge of human behavior, cognition, physical capabilities and dimensions to the design of products, equipment, or large-scale systems that can be used easily, effectively and safely by human operators.
Attention	Attention is the cognitive process of selectively concentrating on one thing while ignoring other things. Psychologists have labeled three types of attention: sustained attention, selective attention, and divided attention.

Aptitude test	A test designed to predict a person's ability in a particular area or line of work is called an aptitude test.
Hawthorne effect	The Hawthorne effect refers to improvements in productivity or quality which result not so much because of intended changes to working conditions, but mainly because the workers are aware of extra attention being paid to them.
Applied psychology	The basic premise of applied psychology is the use of psychological principles and theories to overcome practical problems.
Discrimination	In Learning theory, discrimination refers the ability to distinguish between a conditioned stimulus and other stimuli. It can be brought about by extensive training or differential reinforcement. In social terms, it is the denial of privileges to a person or a group on the basis of prejudice.
Gender difference	A gender difference is a disparity between genders involving quality or quantity. Though some gender differences are controversial, they are not to be confused with sexist stereotypes.
Statistics	Statistics is a type of data analysis which practice includes the planning, summarizing, and interpreting of observations of a system possibly followed by predicting or forecasting of future events based on a mathematical model of the system being observed.
Statistic	A statistic is an observable random variable of a sample.
Scientific research	Research that is objective, systematic, and testable is called scientific research.
Individual differences	Individual differences psychology studies the ways in which individual people differ in their behavior. This is distinguished from other aspects of psychology in that although psychology is ostensibly a study of individuals, modern psychologists invariably study groups.
Median	The median is a number that separates the higher half of a sample, a population, or a probability distribution from the lower half. It is the middle value in a distribution, above and below which lie an equal number of values.
Occupational health psychology	An interdisciplinary subfield of psychology concerned with employee health, safety, and well-being is occupational health psychology.
Health psychology	The field of psychology that studies the relationships between psychological factors and the prevention and treatment of physical illness is called health psychology.
Knowledge base	The general background information a person possesses, which influences most cognitive task performance is called the knowledge base.
Ergonomics	Ergonomics refers to the branch of psychology concerned with the interaction of people and technology; also called engineering psychology or human factors.
Affect	A subjective feeling or emotional tone often accompanied by bodily expressions noticeable to others is called affect.

Research method	The scope of the research method is to produce some new knowledge. This, in principle, can take three main forms: Exploratory research; Constructive research; and Empirical research.
Generalizability	The ability to extend a set of findings observed in one piece of research to other situations and groups is called generalizability.
Survey	A method of scientific investigation in which a large sample of people answer questions about their attitudes or behavior is referred to as a survey.
Descriptive statistic	A simple numerical description of observations, such as the mean of a distribution of scores, used to summarize the observations is a descriptive statistic.
Statistic	A statistic is an observable random variable of a sample.
Statistics	Statistics is a type of data analysis which practice includes the planning, summarizing, and interpreting of observations of a system possibly followed by predicting or forecasting of future events based on a mathematical model of the system being observed.
Inferential statistics	Inferential statistics is the branch of statistics that is concerned with the degree of confidence that conclusions drawn about samples can be extended to the populations from which the samples were drawn .
Meta-analysis	In statistics, a meta-analysis combines the results of several studies that address a set of related research hypotheses.
Statistical test	One may be faced with the problem of making a definite decision with respect to an uncertain hypothesis which is known only through its observable consequences. A statistical test is an algorithm to state the alternative (for or against the hypothesis) which minimizes certain risks.
Hawthorne effect	The Hawthorne effect refers to improvements in productivity or quality which result not so much because of intended changes to working conditions, but mainly because the workers are aware of extra attention being paid to them.
Research design	A research design tests a hypothesis. The basic typess are: descriptive, correlational, and experimental.
Reliability	Reliability means the extent to which a test produces a consistent , reproducible score .
Validity	The extent to which a test measures what it is intended to measure is called validity.
Affect	A subjective feeling or emotional tone often accompanied by bodily expressions noticeable to others is called affect.
Hypothesis	A specific statement about behavior or mental processes that is testable through research is a hypothesis.
Theories	Theories are logically self-consistent models or frameworks describing the behavior of a certain natural or social phenomenon. They are broad explanations and predictions concerning phenomena of interest.
Variable	A variable refers to a measurable factor, characteristic, or attribute of an individual or a system.
Attitude	An enduring mental representation of a person, place, or thing that evokes an emotional response and related behavior is called attitude.
Job satisfaction	A person's attitudes and feelings about his or her job and facets of the job is called job satisfaction.
Independent variable	A condition in a scientific study that is manipulated (assigned different values by a researcher) so that the effects of the manipulation may be observed is called an independent

	variable.
Dependent variable	A measure of an assumed effect of an independent variable is called the dependent variable.
Laboratory study	Any research study in which the subjects are brought to a specially designated area that has been set up to facilitate the researcher's ability to control the environment or collect data is referred to as a laboratory study.
Learning	Learning is a relatively permanent change in behavior that results from experience. Thus, to attribute a behavioral change to learning, the change must be relatively permanent and must result from experience.
Laboratory setting	Research setting in which the behavior of interest does not naturally occur is called a laboratory setting.
Control group	A group that does not receive the treatment effect in an experiment is referred to as the control group or sometimes as the comparison group.
Placebo	Placebo refers to a bogus treatment that has the appearance of being genuine.
Field study	Field study refers to any scientific research study in which data are collected in a setting other than the laboratory.
Random selection	Choosing a sample so that each member of the population has an equal chance of being included in the sample is called random selection.
Random assignment	Assignment of participants to experimental and control groups by chance is called random assignment. Random assigment reduces the likelihood that the results are due to preexisiting systematic differences between the groups.
Motivation	In psychology, motivation is the driving force (desire) behind all actions of an organism.
Random sample	A sample drawn so that each member of a population has an equal chance of being selected to participate is referred to as a random sample.
Confounding variable	A confounding variable is a variable which is the common cause of two things that may falsely appear to be in a causal relationship. It is the cause of a spurious relationship.
Field experiment	A field experiment applies the scientific method to experimentally examine an intervention in the real world rather than in the laboratory. Field experiments generally randomize subjects into treatment and control groups and compare outcomes between these groups.
Cross-sectional design	A research design in which investigators compare groups of subjects of differing age on some variable is a cross-sectional design.
Longitudinal design	A research design in which investigators observe one group of subjects repeatedly over a period of time is called a longitudinal design.
Response rate	The response rate is usually calculated by dividing the total number of responses by the time available for the response.
Creativity	Creativity is the ability to think about something in novel and unusual ways and come up with unique solutions to problems. It involves divergent thinking, having many solutions or views to a problem.
Categorical measurement	In categorical measurement numbers represent arbitrary categories or names of a variable rather than quantitative positions along a continuum.
Continuous measurement	A continuous measurement technique uses numbers to represent an underlying continuum of a variable from low to high values.
Classical	Classical measurement theory states that a measure is composed of a true score component and

Go to **Cram101.com** for the Practice Tests for this Chapter.

measurement theory	an error component.
Personality	Personality refers to the pattern of enduring characteristics that differentiates a person, the patterns of behaviors that make each individual unique.
Internal consistency reliability	Internal consistency reliability is the level of agreement among the items in a test and the level of agreement of multiple ratings by different raters.
Psychological test	Psychological test refers to a standardized measure of a sample of a person's behavior.
Inter-rater reliability	The degree of the association between the ratings of two raters who rate the same subject on the same variable is inter-rater reliability.
Test-retest reliability	The consistency of a measure when it is repeated over time is called test-retest reliability. It involves administering the test to the same group of people at least twice. The first set of scores is correlated with the second set of scores. Correlations range between 0 (low reliability) and 1 (high reliability).
Intelligence test	An intelligence test is a standardized means of assessing a person's current mental ability, for example, the Stanford-Binet test and the Wechsler Adult Intelligence Scale.
Construct validity	The extent to which there is evidence that a test measures a particular hypothetical construct is referred to as construct validity.
Construct	A generalized concept, such as anxiety or gravity, is a construct.
Face validity	Condition of testing in which test items appear plausible for their intended purposes is called face validity.
Content validity	The degree to which the content of a test is representative of the domain it's supposed to cover is referred to as its content validity.
Criterion-related validity	Test validity that is estimated by correlating subjects' scores on a test with their scores on an independent criterion of the variable assessed by the test is referred to as criterion-related validity.
Central tendency	In statistics, central tendency is an average of a set of measurements, the word average being variously construed as mean, median, or other measure of location, depending on the context. Central tendency is a descriptive statistic analogous to center of mass in physical terms.
Arithmetic mean	The arithmetic mean is the sum of the scores divided by the number of scores.
Median	The median is a number that separates the higher half of a sample, a population, or a probability distribution from the lower half. It is the middle value in a distribution, above and below which lie an equal number of values.
Variance	The degree to which scores differ among individuals in a distribution of scores is the variance.
Standard deviation	In probability and statistics, the standard deviation is the most commonly used measure of statistical dispersion. Simply put, it measures how spread out the values in a data set are.
Correlation	A statistical technique for determining the degree of association between two or more variables is referred to as correlation.
Correlation coefficient	Correlation coefficient refers to a number from +1.00 to -1.00 that expresses the direction and extent of the relationship between two variables. The closer to 1, the stronger the relationship. The sign, + or -, indicates the direction.

Negative correlation	A negative correlation refers to a relationship between two variables in which one variable increases as the other decreases.
Regression equation	A regression equation refers to a mathematical relationship where one variable is predictable from another.
Regression	Return to a form of behavior characteristic of an earlier stage of development is called regression.
Aptitude test	A test designed to predict a person's ability in a particular area or line of work is called an aptitude test.
Multiple regression	A multiple regression is a linear regression with more than one covariate (predictor variable). It can be viewed as a simple case of canonical correlation.
Population	Population refers to all members of a well-defined group of organisms, events, or things.
Variability	Statistically, variability refers to how much the scores in a distribution spread out, away from the mean.
Statistical significance	The condition that exists when the probability that the observed findings are due to chance is very low is called statistical significance.
Analysis of variance	Analysis of variance is an inferential statistical technique used to compare differences between two or more groups with the purpose of making a decision whether the groups come from the same population or not.
Factorial design	A factorial design experiment is a statistical study in which each observation is categorized according to more than one factor. Such an experiment allows studying the effect of each factor on the response variable, while requiring fewer observations than by conducting separate experiments for each factor independently. It also allows studying the effect of the interaction between factors on the response variable.
Negative feedback	In negative feedback, the output of a system is added back into the input, so as to reverse the direction of change. This tends to keep the output from changing, so it is stabilizing and attempts to maintain homeostasis.
Feedback	Feedback refers to information returned to a person about the effects a response has had.
Informed consent	The term used by psychologists to indicate that a person has agreed to participate in research after receiving information about the purposes of the study and the nature of the treatments is informed consent. Even with informed consent, subjects may withdraw from any experiment at any time.

Job components	A job components inventory is a method of job analysis that matches job requirements to characteristics of people.
Validity	The extent to which a test measures what it is intended to measure is called validity.
Perception	Perception is the process of acquiring, interpreting, selecting, and organizing sensory information.
Reliability	Reliability means the extent to which a test produces a consistent , reproducible score .
Job evaluation	A job evaluation is to a mathematical procedure for determining the relative value of a job to an organization.
Discrimination	In Learning theory, discrimination refers the ability to distinguish between a conditioned stimulus and other stimuli. It can be brought about by extensive training or differential reinforcement. In social terms, it is the denial of privileges to a person or a group on the basis of prejudice.
Psychological test	Psychological test refers to a standardized measure of a sample of a person's behavior.
Motivation	In psychology, motivation is the driving force (desire) behind all actions of an organism.
Individual differences	Individual differences psychology studies the ways in which individual people differ in their behavior. This is distinguished from other aspects of psychology in that although psychology is ostensibly a study of individuals, modern psychologists invariably study groups.
Anxiety	Anxiety is a complex combination of the feeling of fear, apprehension and worry often accompanied by physical sensations such as palpitations, chest pain and/or shortness of breath.
Personality	Personality refers to the pattern of enduring characteristics that differentiates a person, the patterns of behaviors that make each individual unique.
Questionnaire	A self-report method of data collection or clinical assessment method in which the individual being studied checks off items on a printed list, answers multiple-choice questions, or writes out answers to essay questions aimed at producing a selfdescription is called questionnaire.
Variable	A variable refers to a measurable factor, characteristic, or attribute of an individual or a system.
Survey	A method of scientific investigation in which a large sample of people answer questions about their attitudes or behavior is referred to as a survey.
Insight	Insight refers to a sudden awareness of the relationships among various elements that had previously appeared to be independent of one another.
Attention	Attention is the cognitive process of selectively concentrating on one thing while ignoring other things. Psychologists have labeled three types of attention: sustained attention, selective attention, and divided attention.
Learning	Learning is a relatively permanent change in behavior that results from experience. Thus, to attribute a behavioral change to learning, the change must be relatively permanent and must result from experience.
Reaction time	The amount of time required to respond to a stimulus is referred to as reaction time.
Percentile score	A figure that indicates the percentage of people who score below the score the individual of interest has obtained, is called the percentile score.
Applied	The basic premise of applied psychology is the use of psychological principles and theories

psychology	to overcome practical problems.
Information processing	Information processing is an approach to the goal of understanding human thinking. The essence of the approach is to see cognition as being essentially computational in nature, with mind being the software and the brain being the hardware.
Visual acuity	Visual acuity is the eye's ability to detect fine details and is the quantitative measure of the eye's ability to see an in-focus image at a certain distance.
Preparedness	The species-specific biological predisposition to learn in certain ways is called preparedness.
Correlation	A statistical technique for determining the degree of association between two or more variables is referred to as correlation.
Affect	A subjective feeling or emotional tone often accompanied by bodily expressions noticeable to others is called affect.
Modeling	A type of behavior learned through observation of others demonstrating the same behavior is modeling.

Feedback	Feedback refers to information returned to a person about the effects a response has had.
Affect	A subjective feeling or emotional tone often accompanied by bodily expressions noticeable to others is called affect.
Anxiety	Anxiety is a complex combination of the feeling of fear, apprehension and worry often accompanied by physical sensations such as palpitations, chest pain and/or shortness of breath.
Control group	A group that does not receive the treatment effect in an experiment is referred to as the control group or sometimes as the comparison group.
Construct	A generalized concept, such as anxiety or gravity, is a construct.
Actual criterion	Actual criterion refers to the way in which the theoretical criterion is assessed; the operationalization of a construct.
Achievement test	A test designed to determine a person's level of knowledge in a given subject area is referred to as an achievement test.
Criterion contamination	The extent to which an actual criterion assesses something other than the theoretical criterion is referred to as criterion contamination.
Criterion deficiency	Criterion deficiency refers to the extent to which a theoretical criterion is not assessed by the actual criterion.
Criterion relevance	The extent to which the actual criterion assesses the theoretical criterion are called the criterion relevance.
Content validity	The degree to which the content of a test is representative of the domain it's supposed to cover is referred to as its content validity.
Validity	The extent to which a test measures what it is intended to measure is called validity.
Test battery	A group of tests and interviews given to the same individual is a test battery.
Construct validity	The extent to which there is evidence that a test measures a particular hypothetical construct is referred to as construct validity.
Variable	A variable refers to a measurable factor, characteristic, or attribute of an individual or a system.
Variability	Statistically, variability refers to how much the scores in a distribution spread out, away from the mean.
Incentive	An incentive is what is expected once a behavior is performed. An incentive acts as a reinforcer.
Standard deviation	In probability and statistics, the standard deviation is the most commonly used measure of statistical dispersion. Simply put, it measures how spread out the values in a data set are.
Clone	A clone is a genetic, not behavioral, copy of an organism.
Trait	An enduring personality characteristic that tends to lead to certain behaviors is called a trait. The term trait also means a genetically inherited feature of an organism.
Attitude	An enduring mental representation of a person, place, or thing that evokes an emotional response and related behavior is called attitude.
Motivation	In psychology, motivation is the driving force (desire) behind all actions of an organism.
Schemata	Cognitive categories or frames of reference are called schemata.
Schema	Schema refers to a way of mentally representing the world, such as a belief or an

expectation, that can influence perception of persons, objects, and situations.

Prototype	A concept of a category of objects or events that serves as a good example of the category is called a prototype.
Priming	A phenomenon in which exposure to a word or concept later makes it easier to recall related information, even when one has no conscious memory of the word or concept is called priming.
Halo error	The tendency for a rater to give an individual the same rating across different dimensions of performance is called the halo error.
True halo	The extent to which a person's performance across different dimensions is at the same level is called true halo.
Central tendency	In statistics, central tendency is an average of a set of measurements, the word average being variously construed as mean, median, or other measure of location, depending on the context. Central tendency is a descriptive statistic analogous to center of mass in physical terms.
Leniency error	The tendency for a rater to give everyone high ratings across dimensions of performance is called a leniency error.
Attention	Attention is the cognitive process of selectively concentrating on one thing while ignoring other things. Psychologists have labeled three types of attention: sustained attention, selective attention, and divided attention.
Perception	Perception is the process of acquiring, interpreting, selecting, and organizing sensory information.
Laboratory study	Any research study in which the subjects are brought to a specially designated area that has been set up to facilitate the researcher's ability to control the environment or collect data is referred to as a laboratory study.
Information processing	Information processing is an approach to the goal of understanding human thinking. The essence of the approach is to see cognition as being essentially computational in nature, with mind being the software and the brain being the hardware.
Discrimination	In Learning theory, discrimination refers the ability to distinguish between a conditioned stimulus and other stimuli. It can be brought about by extensive training or differential reinforcement. In social terms, it is the denial of privileges to a person or a group on the basis of prejudice.

Personality	Personality refers to the pattern of enduring characteristics that differentiates a person, the patterns of behaviors that make each individual unique.
Psychological test	Psychological test refers to a standardized measure of a sample of a person's behavior.
Learning	Learning is a relatively permanent change in behavior that results from experience. Thus, to attribute a behavioral change to learning, the change must be relatively permanent and must result from experience.
Reliability	Reliability means the extent to which a test produces a consistent , reproducible score .
Validity	The extent to which a test measures what it is intended to measure is called validity.
Attitude	An enduring mental representation of a person, place, or thing that evokes an emotional response and related behavior is called attitude.
Personality test	A personality test aims to describe aspects of a person's character that remain stable across situations.
Power test	A test without a time limit is referred to as a power test.
Information processing	Information processing is an approach to the goal of understanding human thinking. The essence of the approach is to see cognition as being essentially computational in nature, with mind being the software and the brain being the hardware.
Reasoning	Reasoning is the act of using reason to derive a conclusion from certain premises. There are two main methods to reach a conclusion,deductive reasoning and inductive reasoning.
Intelligence test	An intelligence test is a standardized means of assessing a person's current mental ability, for example, the Stanford-Binet test and the Wechsler Adult Intelligence Scale.
Problem solving	An attempt to find an appropriate way of attaining a goal when the goal is not readily available is called problem solving.
Coding	In senation, coding is the process by which information about the quality and quantity of a stimulus is preserved in the pattern of action potentials sent through sensory neurons to the central nervous system.
Achievement test	A test designed to determine a person's level of knowledge in a given subject area is referred to as an achievement test.
Psychomotor ability test	A psychomotor ability test assesses physical-mental abilities, such as eye-hand coordination.
Personality trait	According to the Diagnostic and Statistical Manual of the American Psychiatric Association, a personality trait is a "prominent aspect of personality that is exhibited in a wide range of important social and personal contexts. ...".
Trait	An enduring personality characteristic that tends to lead to certain behaviors is called a trait. The term trait also means a genetically inherited feature of an organism.
Predisposition	Predisposition refers to an inclination or diathesis to respond in a certain way, either inborn or acquired. In abnormal psychology, it is a factor that lowers the ability to withstand stress and inclines the individual toward pathology.
Anxiety	Anxiety is a complex combination of the feeling of fear, apprehension and worry often accompanied by physical sensations such as palpitations, chest pain and/or shortness of breath.
Emotional intelligence	The expression emotional intelligence indicates a kind of intelligence or skill that involves the ability to perceive, assess and positively influence one's own and other people's

emotions.

Emotion	An emotion is a mental states that arise spontaneously, rather than through conscious effort. They are often accompanied by physiological changes.
Construct	A generalized concept, such as anxiety or gravity, is a construct.
Emotional regulation	Techniques for controlling one's emotional states to efficiently adapt and reach a goal is called emotional regulation.
Guilt	Guilt describes many concepts related to a negative emotion or condition caused by actions which are believed to be, morally wrong. According to Freud, the avoidance of guilt is the basis for moral behavior.
Counselor	A counselor is a mental health professional who specializes in helping people with problems not involving serious mental disorders.
Clinical psychologist	A psychologist, usually with a Ph.D, whose training is in the diagnosis, treatment, or research of psychological and behavioral disorders is a clinical psychologist.
Empirical	Empirical means the use of working hypotheses which are capable of being disproved using observation or experiment.
Empirical biographical inventory	A biographical inventory developed statistically by conducting analyses of a large number of items to see which ones predict job performance is referred to as the empirical biographical inventory.
Personality inventory	A self-report questionnaire by which an examinee indicates whether statements assessing habitual tendencies apply to him or her is referred to as a personality inventory.
Extraversion	Extraversion, one of the big-five personailty traits, is marked by pronounced engagement with the external world. They are people who enjoy being with people, are full of energy, and often experience positive emotions.
Agreeableness	Agreeableness, one of the big-five personality traits, reflects individual differences in concern with cooperation and social harmony. It is the degree individuals value getting along with others.
Conscientiou-ness	Conscientiousness is one of the dimensions of the five-factor model of personality and individual differences involving being organized, thorough, and reliable as opposed to careless, negligent, and unreliable.
Motivation	In psychology, motivation is the driving force (desire) behind all actions of an organism.
Variable	A variable refers to a measurable factor, characteristic, or attribute of an individual or a system.
Correlation	A statistical technique for determining the degree of association between two or more variables is referred to as correlation.
Generalizability	The ability to extend a set of findings observed in one piece of research to other situations and groups is called generalizability.
Structured interview	Structured interview refers to an interview in which the questions are set out in a prescribed fashion for the interviewer. It assists professionals in making diagnostic decisions based upon standardized criteria.
Affect	A subjective feeling or emotional tone often accompanied by bodily expressions noticeable to others is called affect.
Questionnaire	A self-report method of data collection or clinical assessment method in which the individual being studied checks off items on a printed list, answers multiple-choice questions, or

	writes out answers to essay questions aimed at producing a selfdescription is called questionnaire.
Wisdom	Wisdom is the ability to make correct judgments and decisions. It is an intangible quality gained through experience. Whether or not something is wise is determined in a pragmatic sense by its popularity, how long it has been around, and its ability to predict against future events.
Meta-analysis	In statistics, a meta-analysis combines the results of several studies that address a set of related research hypotheses.
Insight	Insight refers to a sudden awareness of the relationships among various elements that had previously appeared to be independent of one another.
Simulation	A simulation is an imitation of some real device or state of affairs. Simulation attempts to represent certain features of the behavior of a physical or abstract system by the behavior of another system.
Survey	A method of scientific investigation in which a large sample of people answer questions about their attitudes or behavior is referred to as a survey.
Role-play	A training technique that involves having the trainee pretend to perform a task is called role-play.
Leaderless group exercise	An assessment center exercise which monitors the a group without a leader to observe their interpersonal behavior is referred to as the leaderless group exercise.
Applied psychology	The basic premise of applied psychology is the use of psychological principles and theories to overcome practical problems.
Feedback	Feedback refers to information returned to a person about the effects a response has had.
Construct validity	The extent to which there is evidence that a test measures a particular hypothetical construct is referred to as construct validity.

Go to **Cram101.com** for the Practice Tests for this Chapter.

Discrimination	In Learning theory, discrimination refers the ability to distinguish between a conditioned stimulus and other stimuli. It can be brought about by extensive training or differential reinforcement. In social terms, it is the denial of privileges to a person or a group on the basis of prejudice.
Affect	A subjective feeling or emotional tone often accompanied by bodily expressions noticeable to others is called affect.
Projection	Attributing one's own undesirable thoughts, impulses, traits, or behaviors to others is referred to as projection.
Learning	Learning is a relatively permanent change in behavior that results from experience. Thus, to attribute a behavioral change to learning, the change must be relatively permanent and must result from experience.
Statistics	Statistics is a type of data analysis which practice includes the planning, summarizing, and interpreting of observations of a system possibly followed by predicting or forecasting of future events based on a mathematical model of the system being observed.
Statistic	A statistic is an observable random variable of a sample.
Applied psychology	The basic premise of applied psychology is the use of psychological principles and theories to overcome practical problems.
Criterion-related validity	Test validity that is estimated by correlating subjects' scores on a test with their scores on an independent criterion of the variable assessed by the test is referred to as criterion-related validity.
Validity	The extent to which a test measures what it is intended to measure is called validity.
Variable	A variable refers to a measurable factor, characteristic, or attribute of an individual or a system.
Statistical test	One may be faced with the problem of making a definite decision with respect to an uncertain hypothesis which is known only through its observable consequences. A statistical test is an algorithm to state the alternative (for or against the hypothesis) which minimizes certain risks.
Correlation coefficient	Correlation coefficient refers to a number from +1.00 to -1.00 that expresses the direction and extent of the relationship between two variables. The closer to 1, the stronger the relationship. The sign, + or -, indicates the direction.
Correlation	A statistical technique for determining the degree of association between two or more variables is referred to as correlation.
Psychological test	Psychological test refers to a standardized measure of a sample of a person's behavior.
Job satisfaction	A person's attitudes and feelings about his or her job and facets of the job is called job satisfaction.
Generalization	In conditioning, the tendency for a conditioned response to be evoked by stimuli that are similar to the stimulus to which the response was conditioned is a generalization. The greater the similarity among the stimuli, the greater the probability of generalization.
Concurrent validation study	A validation strategy in which the predictor and criterion are assessed at the same time is a concurrent validation study.
Predictive validity study	A predictive validity study is a design in which predictor information is used to forecast a criterion that is assessed at a later time .

Predictive validity	Predictive validity refers to the relation between test scores and the student 's future performance .
Generalizability	The ability to extend a set of findings observed in one piece of research to other situations and groups is called generalizability.
Cross-validate	To cross-validate is to replicate the results of one sample with those of another sample.
Validity generalization	A principle that states that if a predictor is a valid indicator of a criterion in one setting, it will be valid in another similar setting is the validity generalization.
Regression equation	A regression equation refers to a mathematical relationship where one variable is predictable from another.
Regression	Return to a form of behavior characteristic of an earlier stage of development is called regression.
Multiple hurdle	A multiple hurdle is a selection method whereby applicants must achieve a certain score on each predictor in order to be selected.
Multiple regression	A multiple regression is a linear regression with more than one covariate (predictor variable). It can be viewed as a simple case of canonical correlation.
Trait	An enduring personality characteristic that tends to lead to certain behaviors is called a trait. The term trait also means a genetically inherited feature of an organism.
Simulation	A simulation is an imitation of some real device or state of affairs. Simulation attempts to represent certain features of the behavior of a physical or abstract system by the behavior of another system.
Survey	A method of scientific investigation in which a large sample of people answer questions about their attitudes or behavior is referred to as a survey.
Field experiment	A field experiment applies the scientific method to experimentally examine an intervention in the real world rather than in the laboratory. Field experiments generally randomize subjects into treatment and control groups and compare outcomes between these groups.
Meta-analysis	In statistics, a meta-analysis combines the results of several studies that address a set of related research hypotheses.
Reflection	Reflection is the process of rephrasing or repeating thoughts and feelings expressed, making the person more aware of what they are saying or thinking.
Feedback	Feedback refers to information returned to a person about the effects a response has had.
Personality	Personality refers to the pattern of enduring characteristics that differentiates a person, the patterns of behaviors that make each individual unique.
Threshold	In general, a threshold is a fixed location or value where an abrupt change is observed. In the sensory modalities, it is the minimum amount of stimulus energy necessary to elicit a sensory response.
Reasonable accommodation	A principle from the Americans With Disabilities Act that requires organizations to provide reasonable assistance or modifications to the job or workplace so that people with disabilities can perform the job is called reasonable accommodation.
Accommodation	Piaget's developmental process of accommodation is the modification of currently held schemes or new schemes so that new information inconsistent with the existing schemes can be integrated and understood.
Reverse discrimination	Reverse discrimination is a term used to describe discriminatory policies or acts that benefit a historically sociopolitically nondominant group (typically minorities), rather than

Go to **Cram101.com** for the Practice Tests for this Chapter.

	the historically sociopolitically dominant group.
Attitude	An enduring mental representation of a person, place, or thing that evokes an emotional response and related behavior is called attitude.
Population	Population refers to all members of a well-defined group of organisms, events, or things.
Creativity	Creativity is the ability to think about something in novel and unusual ways and come up with unique solutions to problems. It involves divergent thinking, having many solutions or views to a problem.
Structured interview	Structured interview refers to an interview in which the questions are set out in a prescribed fashion for the interviewer. It assists professionals in making diagnostic decisions based upon standardized criteria.

32

Go to **Cram101.com** for the Practice Tests for this Chapter.

Learning	Learning is a relatively permanent change in behavior that results from experience. Thus, to attribute a behavioral change to learning, the change must be relatively permanent and must result from experience.
Affect	A subjective feeling or emotional tone often accompanied by bodily expressions noticeable to others is called affect.
Transfer of training	The concept of transfer of training states that knowledge or abilities acquired in one area aids the acquisition of knowledge or abilities in other areas. When prior learning is helpful, it is called positive transfer. When prior learning inhibits new learning, it is called negative transfer.
Survey	A method of scientific investigation in which a large sample of people answer questions about their attitudes or behavior is referred to as a survey.
Individual differences	Individual differences psychology studies the ways in which individual people differ in their behavior. This is distinguished from other aspects of psychology in that although psychology is ostensibly a study of individuals, modern psychologists invariably study groups.
Simulation	A simulation is an imitation of some real device or state of affairs. Simulation attempts to represent certain features of the behavior of a physical or abstract system by the behavior of another system.
Attitude	An enduring mental representation of a person, place, or thing that evokes an emotional response and related behavior is called attitude.
Motivation	In psychology, motivation is the driving force (desire) behind all actions of an organism.
Meta-analysis	In statistics, a meta-analysis combines the results of several studies that address a set of related research hypotheses.
Feedback	Feedback refers to information returned to a person about the effects a response has had.
Identical elements	Thorndike's theory suggests that transfer of learning depends upon the presence of identical elements in the original and new learning situations; i.e., transfer is always specific, never general. In later versions of the theory, the concept of "belongingness" was introduced; connections are more readily established if the person perceives that stimuli or responses go together.
Overlearning	Continued rehearsal of material after one first appears to have mastered it is called overlearning.
Automaticity	The ability to process information with little or no effort is referred to as automaticity.
Attention	Attention is the cognitive process of selectively concentrating on one thing while ignoring other things. Psychologists have labeled three types of attention: sustained attention, selective attention, and divided attention.
Part training	Part training is the training of individual subtasks one at a time.
Whole training	Whole training focuses on an entire task at one time rather than on parts of the task.
Applied psychology	The basic premise of applied psychology is the use of psychological principles and theories to overcome practical problems.
Modeling	A type of behavior learned through observation of others demonstrating the same behavior is modeling.
Role-playing	Role-playing refers to a technique that teaches people to behave in a certain way by encouraging them to pretend that they are in a particular situation; it helps people acquire complex behaviors in an efficient way.

Programmed instruction	Programmed instruction is characterized by clearly stated behavioral objectives, small frames of instruction, self-pacing, active learner response to inserted questions, and immediate feedback regarding the correctness of a response.
Negative feedback	In negative feedback, the output of a system is added back into the input, so as to reverse the direction of change. This tends to keep the output from changing, so it is stabilizing and attempts to maintain homeostasis.
Role-play	A training technique that involves having the trainee pretend to perform a task is called role-play.
Mentoring	Mentoring refers to a developmental relationship between a more experienced individual and a less experienced partner sometimes referred to as a protégé. In well-designed formal mentoring programs, there are program goals, schedules, and training.
Questionnaire	A self-report method of data collection or clinical assessment method in which the individual being studied checks off items on a printed list, answers multiple-choice questions, or writes out answers to essay questions aimed at producing a selfdescription is called questionnaire.
Personality test	A personality test aims to describe aspects of a person's character that remain stable across situations.
Personality	Personality refers to the pattern of enduring characteristics that differentiates a person, the patterns of behaviors that make each individual unique.
Extraversion	Extraversion, one of the big-five personailty traits, is marked by pronounced engagement with the external world. They are people who enjoy being with people, are full of energy, and often experience positive emotions.
Correlation	A statistical technique for determining the degree of association between two or more variables is referred to as correlation.
Antecedents	In behavior modification, events that typically precede the target response are called antecedents.
Research design	A research design tests a hypothesis. The basic typess are: descriptive, correlational, and experimental.
Field experiment	A field experiment applies the scientific method to experimentally examine an intervention in the real world rather than in the laboratory. Field experiments generally randomize subjects into treatment and control groups and compare outcomes between these groups.
Control group	A group that does not receive the treatment effect in an experiment is referred to as the control group or sometimes as the comparison group.
Pretest-posttest design	A pretest-posttest design examines the same criterion variable before and after the treatment occurs.
Random assignment	Assignment of participants to experimental and control groups by chance is called random assignment. Random assigment reduces the likelihood that the results are due to preexisiting systematic differences between the groups.
Inferential statistics	Inferential statistics is the branch of statistics that is concerned with the degree of confidence that conclusions drawn about samples can be extended to the populations from which the samples were drawn .
Statistics	Statistics is a type of data analysis which practice includes the planning, summarizing, and interpreting of observations of a system possibly followed by predicting or forecasting of future events based on a mathematical model of the system being observed.

Go to **Cram101.com** for the Practice Tests for this Chapter.

Statistic	A statistic is an observable random variable of a sample.
Structured interview	Structured interview refers to an interview in which the questions are set out in a prescribed fashion for the interviewer. It assists professionals in making diagnostic decisions based upon standardized criteria.

38

Go to **Cram101.com** for the Practice Tests for this Chapter.

Theories	Theories are logically self-consistent models or frameworks describing the behavior of a certain natural or social phenomenon. They are broad explanations and predictions concerning phenomena of interest.
Motivation	In psychology, motivation is the driving force (desire) behind all actions of an organism.
Variable	A variable refers to a measurable factor, characteristic, or attribute of an individual or a system.
Affect	A subjective feeling or emotional tone often accompanied by bodily expressions noticeable to others is called affect.
Work motivation	The conditions and processes responsible for the arousal, direction, magnitude, and maintenance of effort one puts forth in one's job is called the work motivation.
Validity	The extent to which a test measures what it is intended to measure is called validity.
Reinforcement Theory	Reinforcement theory holds that reinforcers can control behavior. The definition has two main components: Contingency, where the occurrence of the reinforcer depends on the occurrence of the learner's response, and Rate of Responding, where the reinforcer serves to increase the learner's rate of responding.
Reinforcement	In operant conditioning, reinforcement is any change in an environment that (a) occurs after the behavior, (b) seems to make that behavior re-occur more often in the future and (c) that reoccurence of behavior must be the result of the change.
Motives	Needs or desires that energize and direct behavior toward a goal are motives.
Expectancy theory	According to the expectancy theory the amount of effort people exert on a specific task depends on their expectations of the outcome.
Attention	Attention is the cognitive process of selectively concentrating on one thing while ignoring other things. Psychologists have labeled three types of attention: sustained attention, selective attention, and divided attention.
Self-actualization	Self-actualization (a term originated by Kurt Goldstein) is the instinctual need of a human to make the most of their unique abilities. Maslow described it as follows: Self Actualization is the intrinsic growth of what is already in the organism, or more accurately, of what the organism is.
Punishment	Punishment is the addtion of a stimulus that reduces the frequency of a response, or the removal of a stimulus that results in a reduction of the response.
Empirical	Empirical means the use of working hypotheses which are capable of being disproved using observation or experiment.
Growth needs	Maslow's hierarchy of needs is often depicted as a pyramid consisting of five levels: the four lower levels are grouped together as deficiency needs, while the top level is termed growth needs, those of self-actualization.
Creativity	Creativity is the ability to think about something in novel and unusual ways and come up with unique solutions to problems. It involves divergent thinking, having many solutions or views to a problem.
Frustration-regression	The frustration-regression principle of ERG theory says that people will revert to a lower-level need when fulfillment of a higher-level need is blocked.
Hygiene factors	Hygiene factors are job factors that can cause dissatisfaction if missing but do not necessarily motivate employees if increased.
Job satisfaction	A person's attitudes and feelings about his or her job and facets of the job is called job satisfaction.

Enrichment	Deliberately making an environment more novel, complex, and perceptually or intellectually stimulating is referred to as enrichment.
Law of effect	The law of effect is a principle of psychology described by Edward Thorndike in 1898. It holds that responses to stimuli that produce a satisfying or pleasant effect in a particular situation are more likely to occur again in the situation. Conversely, responses that produce a discomforting or unpleasant effect are less likely to occur again in the situation
Incentive	An incentive is what is expected once a behavior is performed. An incentive acts as a reinforcer.
Piece-rate system	A system that pays employees for each unit of productivity is called a piece-rate system.
Meta-analysis	In statistics, a meta-analysis combines the results of several studies that address a set of related research hypotheses.
Insight	Insight refers to a sudden awareness of the relationships among various elements that had previously appeared to be independent of one another.
Motivational processes	In observational learning, the motivational processes are the degree to which a behavior is seen to result in a valued outcome (expectancies) will influence the likelihood that one will adopt a modeled behavior .
Self-esteem	Self-esteem refers to a person's subjective appraisal of himself or herself as intrinsically positive or negative to some degree.
Valence	In expectancy theory, the value or worth a person gives to an outcome is called the valence.
Instrumentality	In expectancy theory, the belief that performance will lead to rewards is called instrumentality.
Self-efficacy	Self-efficacy is the belief that one has the capabilities to execute the courses of actions required to manage prospective situations.
Self-fulfilling prophecy	A self-fulfilling prophecy is a prediction that, in being made, actually causes itself to become true.
Self-efficacy theory	Self-efficacy theory is a motivation theory based on the idea that people perform well when they believe they are capable of doing the job.
Longitudinal study	Longitudinal study is a type of developmental study in which the same group of participants is followed and measured for an extended period of time, often years.
Correlation	A statistical technique for determining the degree of association between two or more variables is referred to as correlation.
Simulation	A simulation is an imitation of some real device or state of affairs. Simulation attempts to represent certain features of the behavior of a physical or abstract system by the behavior of another system.
Feedback	Feedback refers to information returned to a person about the effects a response has had.
Galatea effect	A type of self-fulfilling prophecy in which a belief in being able to do something well results in better performance by an individual is the called galatea effect.
Control group	A group that does not receive the treatment effect in an experiment is referred to as the control group or sometimes as the comparison group.
Role-play	A training technique that involves having the trainee pretend to perform a task is called role-play.
Transfer of	The concept of transfer of training states that knowledge or abilities acquired in one area

Go to **Cram101.com** for the Practice Tests for this Chapter.

training	aids the acquisition of knowledge or abilities in other areas. When prior learning is helpful, it is called positive transfer. When prior learning inhibits new learning, it is called negative transfer.
Applied psychology	The basic premise of applied psychology is the use of psychological principles and theories to overcome practical problems.
Guilt	Guilt describes many concepts related to a negative emotion or condition caused by actions which are believed to be, morally wrong. According to Freud, the avoidance of guilt is the basis for moral behavior.
Equity theory	Equity theory suggests that people are most satisfied with a relationship when the ratio between benefits and contributions is similar.
Laboratory study	Any research study in which the subjects are brought to a specially designated area that has been set up to facilitate the researcher's ability to control the environment or collect data is referred to as a laboratory study.
Distributive justice	Distributive justice concerns what is just or right with respect to the allocation of goods (or utility) in a society. Distributive justice concentrates on just outcomes.
Procedural justice	Procedural justice concerns the fairness of the processes by which decisions are made.
Anxiety	Anxiety is a complex combination of the feeling of fear, apprehension and worry often accompanied by physical sensations such as palpitations, chest pain and/or shortness of breath.
Depression	In everyday language depression refers to any downturn in mood, which may be relatively transitory and perhaps due to something trivial. This is differentiated from Clinical depression which is marked by symptoms that last two weeks or more and are so severe that they interfere with daily living.
Industrial and organizational psychology	Industrial and organizational psychology is the study of the behavior of people in the workplace. Industrial and organizational psychology attempts to apply psychological results and methods to aid workers and organizations.
Baseline	Measure of a particular behavior or process taken before the introduction of the independent variable or treatment is called the baseline.
Action process	From action theory, a series of steps describing the process by which a person translates desire for something into behavior is called the action process.
Action theory	A motivation theory that links a person's goals to his or her behavior is action theory.
Negative feedback	In negative feedback, the output of a system is added back into the input, so as to reverse the direction of change. This tends to keep the output from changing, so it is stabilizing and attempts to maintain homeostasis.
Personality	Personality refers to the pattern of enduring characteristics that differentiates a person, the patterns of behaviors that make each individual unique.
Cognition	The intellectual processes through which information is obtained, transformed, stored, retrieved, and otherwise used is cognition.

Job satisfaction	A person's attitudes and feelings about his or her job and facets of the job is called job satisfaction.
Questionnaire	A self-report method of data collection or clinical assessment method in which the individual being studied checks off items on a printed list, answers multiple-choice questions, or writes out answers to essay questions aimed at producing a selfdescription is called questionnaire.
Antecedents	In behavior modification, events that typically precede the target response are called antecedents.
Life satisfaction	A person's attitudes about his or her overall life are referred to as life satisfaction.
Emotional labor	Emotional labor is a task that requires someone to suppress or simulate their emotions, particularly related to working conditions.
Variable	A variable refers to a measurable factor, characteristic, or attribute of an individual or a system.
Theories	Theories are logically self-consistent models or frameworks describing the behavior of a certain natural or social phenomenon. They are broad explanations and predictions concerning phenomena of interest.
Organizational commitment	Organizational commitment is the extent of an individual's commitment to an organization. There are three major types of commitment, according to Meyer and Allen's three-component model: Affective Commitment; Continuance Commitment; and Normative Commitment.
Attachment	Attachment is the tendency to seek closeness to another person and feel secure when that person is present.
Survey	A method of scientific investigation in which a large sample of people answer questions about their attitudes or behavior is referred to as a survey.
Norms	In testing, standards of test performance that permit the comparison of one person's score on the test to the scores of others who have taken the same test are referred to as norms.
Individualism	Individualism refers to putting personal goals ahead of group goals and defining one's identity in terms of personal attributes rather than group memberships.
Locus of control	The place to which an individual attributes control over the receiving of reinforcers -either inside or outside the self is referred to as locus of control.
Collectivism	Collectivism is an emphasis on the group, as opposed to the individual. It is syndrome of attitudes and behaviors based on the belief that the basic unit of survival lies within a group, not the individual.
Masculinity	Masculinity is a culturally determined value reflecting the set of characteristics of maleness.
Power distance	Power distance is a cultural index derived by sociologist Geert Hofstede. It measures how much a culture has respect for authority.
Obedience	Obedience is the willingness to follow the will of others. Humans have been shown to be surprisingly obedient in the presence of perceived legitimate authority figures, as demonstrated by the Milgram experiment in the 1960s.
Collectivist	A person who defines the self in terms of relationships to other people and groups and gives priority to group goals is called collectivist.
Validity	The extent to which a test measures what it is intended to measure is called validity.

Go to **Cram101.com** for the Practice Tests for this Chapter.

47

Reliability	Reliability means the extent to which a test produces a consistent , reproducible score .
Correlation	A statistical technique for determining the degree of association between two or more variables is referred to as correlation.
Personality	Personality refers to the pattern of enduring characteristics that differentiates a person, the patterns of behaviors that make each individual unique.
Hypothesis	A specific statement about behavior or mental processes that is testable through research is a hypothesis.
Feedback	Feedback refers to information returned to a person about the effects a response has had.
Meta-analysis	In statistics, a meta-analysis combines the results of several studies that address a set of related research hypotheses.
Job characteristics model	A model that relates employee motivation and satisfaction to job characteristics is called the job characteristics model.
Autonomy	Autonomy is the condition of something that does not depend on anything else.
Hawthorne effect	The Hawthorne effect refers to improvements in productivity or quality which result not so much because of intended changes to working conditions, but mainly because the workers are aware of extra attention being paid to them.
Role conflict	Role conflict is trying to occupy two or more roles that make conflicting demands on behavior.
Work-family conflict	A form of role conflict in which family demands and work demands are at odds is the work-family conflict.
Simulation	A simulation is an imitation of some real device or state of affairs. Simulation attempts to represent certain features of the behavior of a physical or abstract system by the behavior of another system.
Attention	Attention is the cognitive process of selectively concentrating on one thing while ignoring other things. Psychologists have labeled three types of attention: sustained attention, selective attention, and divided attention.
Depression	In everyday language depression refers to any downturn in mood, which may be relatively transitory and perhaps due to something trivial. This is differentiated from Clinical depression which is marked by symptoms that last two weeks or more and are so severe that they interfere with daily living.
Self-esteem	Self-esteem refers to a person's subjective appraisal of himself or herself as intrinsically positive or negative to some degree.
Social support	Social Support is the physical and emotional comfort given by family, friends, co-workers and others. Research has identified three main types of social support: emotional, practical, sharing points of view.
Attitude	An enduring mental representation of a person, place, or thing that evokes an emotional response and related behavior is called attitude.
Procedural justice	Procedural justice concerns the fairness of the processes by which decisions are made.
Identical twins	Identical twins occur when a single egg is fertilized to form one zygote (monozygotic) but the zygote then divides into two separate embryos. The two embryos develop into foetuses sharing the same womb. Monozygotic twins are genetically identical unless there has been a mutation in development, and they are almost always the same gender.

Genetics	Genetics is the science of genes, heredity, and the variation of organisms.
Chronic	Chronic refers to a relatively long duration, usually more than a few months.
Longitudinal study	Longitudinal study is a type of developmental study in which the same group of participants is followed and measured for an extended period of time, often years.
Trait	An enduring personality characteristic that tends to lead to certain behaviors is called a trait. The term trait also means a genetically inherited feature of an organism.
Clinical psychologist	A psychologist, usually with a Ph.D, whose training is in the diagnosis, treatment, or research of psychological and behavioral disorders is a clinical psychologist.
Adolescence	The period of life bounded by puberty and the assumption of adult responsibilities is adolescence.
Emotion	An emotion is a mental states that arise spontaneously, rather than through conscious effort. They are often accompanied by physiological changes.
Anxiety	Anxiety is a complex combination of the feeling of fear, apprehension and worry often accompanied by physical sensations such as palpitations, chest pain and/or shortness of breath.
Gender difference	A gender difference is a disparity between genders involving quality or quantity. Though some gender differences are controversial, they are not to be confused with sexist stereotypes.
Population	Population refers to all members of a well-defined group of organisms, events, or things.
Discrimination	In Learning theory, discrimination refers the ability to distinguish between a conditioned stimulus and other stimuli. It can be brought about by extensive training or differential reinforcement. In social terms, it is the denial of privileges to a person or a group on the basis of prejudice.
Life span	Life span refers to the upper boundary of life, the maximum number of years an individual can live. The maximum life span of human beings is about 120 years of age. Females live an average of 6 years longer than males.
Moderator variable	A variable that affects the relation between two other variables is called the moderator variable.
Statistics	Statistics is a type of data analysis which practice includes the planning, summarizing, and interpreting of observations of a system possibly followed by predicting or forecasting of future events based on a mathematical model of the system being observed.
Statistic	A statistic is an observable random variable of a sample.
Wisdom	Wisdom is the ability to make correct judgments and decisions. It is an intangible quality gained through experience. Whether or not something is wise is determined in a pragmatic sense by its popularity, how long it has been around, and its ability to predict against future events.
Affect	A subjective feeling or emotional tone often accompanied by bodily expressions noticeable to others is called affect.
Compensation	In personaility, compensation, according to Adler, is an effort to overcome imagined or real inferiorities by developing one's abilities.
Positive correlation	A relationship between two variables in which both vary in the same direction is called a positive correlation.
Negative correlation	A negative correlation refers to a relationship between two variables in which one variable increases as the other decreases.

Go to **Cram101.com** for the Practice Tests for this Chapter.

Display rules	Sociocultural standards that determine when, where, and how emotions should be expressed are called display rules.
Emotional dissonance	Emotional dissonance is a feeling experienced when one is forced to fake an emotion.
Continuance Commitment	In Continuance Commitment the individual remains with an organization because of a perceived loss of sunken costs. The individual believes that he has invested a great deal of effort/time and has to remain in the organization.
Normative commitment	In Normative Commitment the individual remains with an organization because of feelings of obligation. For instance, the organization may have invested resources in training an employee who then feels obliged to stay with the organization to repay the debt.
Normative	The term normative is used to describe the effects of those structures of culture which regulate the function of social activity.
Affective Commitment	In Affective Commitment an individual strongly identifies with the goals of the organization and desires to remain a part of the organization. This is the ideal happy state for an individual.
Affective	Affective is the way people react emotionally, their ability to feel another living thing's pain or joy.
Applied psychology	The basic premise of applied psychology is the use of psychological principles and theories to overcome practical problems.
Occupational commitment	Attachment to one's occupation or profession regardless of employer or organization is referred to as occupational commitment.
Negative affectivity	Negative affectivity is a personality variable that refers to a tendency to experience negative emotions across many different situations.

Motivation	In psychology, motivation is the driving force (desire) behind all actions of an organism.
Attention	Attention is the cognitive process of selectively concentrating on one thing while ignoring other things. Psychologists have labeled three types of attention: sustained attention, selective attention, and divided attention.
Human factors	Human factors refers to the study of the interaction of people and machines. It is a technology that applies knowledge of human behavior, cognition, physical capabilities and dimensions to the design of products, equipment, or large-scale systems that can be used easily, effectively and safely by human operators.
Job satisfaction	A person's attitudes and feelings about his or her job and facets of the job is called job satisfaction.
Industrial/organizational psychology	Industrial/organizational psychology is an applied branch of psychology concerned with behavior of individuals and groups in organizations.
Survey	A method of scientific investigation in which a large sample of people answer questions about their attitudes or behavior is referred to as a survey.
Questionnaire	A self-report method of data collection or clinical assessment method in which the individual being studied checks off items on a printed list, answers multiple-choice questions, or writes out answers to essay questions aimed at producing a selfdescription is called questionnaire.
Organizational citizenship behavior	Organizational Citizenship Behavior is a special type of work behavior that are defined as individual behaviors that are beneficial to the organization and are discretionary, not directly or explicitly recognized by the formal reward system.
Organizational constraints	Conditions in an organization that prevent employees from performing well are organizational constraints.
Personality	Personality refers to the pattern of enduring characteristics that differentiates a person, the patterns of behaviors that make each individual unique.
Incentive	An incentive is what is expected once a behavior is performed. An incentive acts as a reinforcer.
Affect	A subjective feeling or emotional tone often accompanied by bodily expressions noticeable to others is called affect.
Reasoning	Reasoning is the act of using reason to derive a conclusion from certain premises. There are two main methods to reach a conclusion,deductive reasoning and inductive reasoning.
Locus of control	The place to which an individual attributes control over the receiving of reinforcers -either inside or outside the self is referred to as locus of control.
Extraversion	Extraversion, one of the big-five personailty traits, is marked by pronounced engagement with the external world. They are people who enjoy being with people, are full of energy, and often experience positive emotions.
Agreeableness	Agreeableness, one of the big-five personality traits, reflects individual differences in concern with cooperation and social harmony. It is the degree individuals value getting along with others.
Conscientiou-ness	Conscientiousness is one of the dimensions of the five-factor model of personality and individual differences involving being organized, thorough, and reliable as opposed to careless, negligent, and unreliable.
Meta-analysis	In statistics, a meta-analysis combines the results of several studies that address a set of

Go to **Cram101.com** for the Practice Tests for this Chapter.

related research hypotheses.

Variable	A variable refers to a measurable factor, characteristic, or attribute of an individual or a system.
Trait	An enduring personality characteristic that tends to lead to certain behaviors is called a trait. The term trait also means a genetically inherited feature of an organism.
Work motivation	The conditions and processes responsible for the arousal, direction, magnitude, and maintenance of effort one puts forth in one's job is called the work motivation.
Stereotype	A stereotype is considered to be a group concept, held by one social group about another. They are often used in a negative or prejudicial sense and are frequently used to justify certain discriminatory behaviors. This allows powerful social groups to legitimize and protect their dominant position
Correlation	A statistical technique for determining the degree of association between two or more variables is referred to as correlation.
Learning	Learning is a relatively permanent change in behavior that results from experience. Thus, to attribute a behavioral change to learning, the change must be relatively permanent and must result from experience.
Wisdom	Wisdom is the ability to make correct judgments and decisions. It is an intangible quality gained through experience. Whether or not something is wise is determined in a pragmatic sense by its popularity, how long it has been around, and its ability to predict against future events.
Theories	Theories are logically self-consistent models or frameworks describing the behavior of a certain natural or social phenomenon. They are broad explanations and predictions concerning phenomena of interest.
Autonomy	Autonomy is the condition of something that does not depend on anything else.
Feedback	Feedback refers to information returned to a person about the effects a response has had.
Job characteristics model	A model that relates employee motivation and satisfaction to job characteristics is called the job characteristics model.
Longitudinal study	Longitudinal study is a type of developmental study in which the same group of participants is followed and measured for an extended period of time, often years.
Reinforcement Theory	Reinforcement theory holds that reinforcers can control behavior. The definition has two main components: Contingency, where the occurrence of the reinforcer depends on the occurrence of the learner's response, and Rate of Responding, where the reinforcer serves to increase the learner's rate of responding.
Reinforcement	In operant conditioning, reinforcement is any change in an environment that (a) occurs after the behavior, (b) seems to make that behavior re-occur more often in the future and (c) that reoccurence of behavior must be the result of the change.
Piece-rate system	A system that pays employees for each unit of productivity is called a piece-rate system.
Ergonomics	Ergonomics refers to the branch of psychology concerned with the interaction of people and technology; also called engineering psychology or human factors.
Engineering psychology	Engineering psychology refers to the branch of psychology concerned with the interaction of people and technology; also called ergonomics or human factors.
Tactile	Pertaining to the sense of touch is referred to as tactile.

Sensation	Sensation is the first stage in the chain of biochemical and neurologic events that begins with the impinging of a stimulus upon the receptor cells of a sensory organ, which then leads to perception, the mental state that is reflected in statements like "I see a uniformly blue wall."
Icon	A mental representation of a visual stimulus that is held briefly in sensory memory is called icon.
Construct	A generalized concept, such as anxiety or gravity, is a construct.
Altruism	Altruism is being helpful to other people with little or no interest in being rewarded for one's efforts. This is distinct from merely helping others.
Applied psychology	The basic premise of applied psychology is the use of psychological principles and theories to overcome practical problems.
Affective Commitment	In Affective Commitment an individual strongly identifies with the goals of the organization and desires to remain a part of the organization. This is the ideal happy state for an individual.
Affective	Affective is the way people react emotionally, their ability to feel another living thing's pain or joy.
Organizational commitment	Organizational commitment is the extent of an individual's commitment to an organization. There are three major types of commitment, according to Meyer and Allen's three-component model: Affective Commitment; Continuance Commitment; and Normative Commitment.
Attitude	An enduring mental representation of a person, place, or thing that evokes an emotional response and related behavior is called attitude.
Work-family conflict	A form of role conflict in which family demands and work demands are at odds is the work-family conflict.
Discrimination	In Learning theory, discrimination refers the ability to distinguish between a conditioned stimulus and other stimuli. It can be brought about by extensive training or differential reinforcement. In social terms, it is the denial of privileges to a person or a group on the basis of prejudice.
Syndrome	The term syndrome is the association of several clinically recognizable features, signs, symptoms, phenomena or characteristics which often occur together, so that the presence of one feature indicates the presence of the others.
Stress management	Stress management encompasses techniques intended to equip a person with effective coping mechanisms for dealing with psychological stress.
Clinical psychology	Clinical psychology is involved in the diagnosis, assessment, and treatment of patients with mental or behavioral disorders, and conducts research in these various areas.
Emotion	An emotion is a mental states that arise spontaneously, rather than through conscious effort. They are often accompanied by physiological changes.
Anxiety	Anxiety is a complex combination of the feeling of fear, apprehension and worry often accompanied by physical sensations such as palpitations, chest pain and/or shortness of breath.
Depression	In everyday language depression refers to any downturn in mood, which may be relatively transitory and perhaps due to something trivial. This is differentiated from Clinical depression which is marked by symptoms that last two weeks or more and are so severe that they interfere with daily living.
Sexual	Deliberate or repeated verbal comments, gestures, or physical contact of a sexual nature that

harassment	is unwanted by the recipient is called sexual harassment.
Negative affectivity	Negative affectivity is a personality variable that refers to a tendency to experience negative emotions across many different situations.
Stress disorder	A significant emotional disturbance caused by stresses outside the range of normal human experience is referred to as stress disorder.

Suicide	Suicide behavior is rare in childhood but escalates in adolescence. The suicide rate increases in a linear fashion from adolescence through late adulthood.
Affect	A subjective feeling or emotional tone often accompanied by bodily expressions noticeable to others is called affect.
Conditioning	Conditioning describes the process by which behaviors can be learned or modified through interaction with the environment.
Variable	A variable refers to a measurable factor, characteristic, or attribute of an individual or a system.
Job satisfaction	A person's attitudes and feelings about his or her job and facets of the job is called job satisfaction.
Attitude	An enduring mental representation of a person, place, or thing that evokes an emotional response and related behavior is called attitude.
Emotion	An emotion is a mental states that arise spontaneously, rather than through conscious effort. They are often accompanied by physiological changes.
Survey	A method of scientific investigation in which a large sample of people answer questions about their attitudes or behavior is referred to as a survey.
Control group	A group that does not receive the treatment effect in an experiment is referred to as the control group or sometimes as the comparison group.
Role conflict	Role conflict is trying to occupy two or more roles that make conflicting demands on behavior.
Organizational constraints	Conditions in an organization that prevent employees from performing well are organizational constraints.
Occupational health psychology	An interdisciplinary subfield of psychology concerned with employee health, safety, and well-being is occupational health psychology.
Health psychology	The field of psychology that studies the relationships between psychological factors and the prevention and treatment of physical illness is called health psychology.
Trauma	Trauma refers to a severe physical injury or wound to the body caused by an external force, or a psychological shock having a lasting effect on mental life.
Anxiety	Anxiety is a complex combination of the feeling of fear, apprehension and worry often accompanied by physical sensations such as palpitations, chest pain and/or shortness of breath.
Cardiovascular disease	Cardiovascular disease refers to afflictions in the mechanisms, including the heart, blood vessels, and their controllers, that are responsible for transporting blood to the body's tissues and organs. Psychological factors may play important roles in such diseases and their treatments.
Statistics	Statistics is a type of data analysis which practice includes the planning, summarizing, and interpreting of observations of a system possibly followed by predicting or forecasting of future events based on a mathematical model of the system being observed.
Statistic	A statistic is an observable random variable of a sample.
Attention	Attention is the cognitive process of selectively concentrating on one thing while ignoring other things. Psychologists have labeled three types of attention: sustained attention, selective attention, and divided attention.

Go to **Cram101.com** for the Practice Tests for this Chapter.

Compensation	In personaility, compensation, according to Adler, is an effort to overcome imagined or real inferiorities by developing one's abilities.
Syndrome	The term syndrome is the association of several clinically recognizable features, signs, symptoms, phenomena or characteristics which often occur together, so that the presence of one feature indicates the presence of the others.
Asthma	Asthma is a complex disease characterized by bronchial hyperresponsiveness (BHR), inflammation, mucus production and intermittent airway obstruction.
Circadian rhythm	The circadian rhythm is a name given to the "internal body clock" that regulates the (roughly) 24 hour cycle of biological processes in animals and plants.
Physiological changes	Alterations in heart rate, blood pressure, perspiration, and other involuntary responses are physiological changes.
Hormone	A hormone is a chemical messenger from one cell (or group of cells) to another. The best known are those produced by endocrine glands, but they are produced by nearly every organ system. The function of hormones is to serve as a signal to the target cells; the action of the hormone is determined by the pattern of secretion and the signal transduction of the receiving tissue.
Stimulant	A stimulant is a drug which increases the activity of the sympathetic nervous system and produces a sense of euphoria or awakeness.
Sleep patterns	The order and timing of daily sleep and waking periods are called sleep patterns.
Questionnaire	A self-report method of data collection or clinical assessment method in which the individual being studied checks off items on a printed list, answers multiple-choice questions, or writes out answers to essay questions aimed at producing a selfdescription is called questionnaire.
Autonomy	Autonomy is the condition of something that does not depend on anything else.
Depression	In everyday language depression refers to any downturn in mood, which may be relatively transitory and perhaps due to something trivial. This is differentiated from Clinical depression which is marked by symptoms that last two weeks or more and are so severe that they interfere with daily living.
Depressant	A depressant is a chemical agent that diminishes a body function or activity. The term is used in particular with regard to the central nervous system where these chemicals are known as neurotransmitters. They tend to act on the CNS by increasing the activity of a particular neurotransmitter known as gamma-aminobutyric acid (GABA).
Correlational study	A correlational study observes or measures two or more variables to find relationships between them. Such studies can identify lawful relationships but cannot determine whether change in one variable is the cause of change in another.
Meta-analysis	In statistics, a meta-analysis combines the results of several studies that address a set of related research hypotheses.
Research design	A research design tests a hypothesis. The basic typess are: descriptive, correlational, and experimental.
Random sample	A sample drawn so that each member of a population has an equal chance of being selected to participate is referred to as a random sample.
Perception	Perception is the process of acquiring, interpreting, selecting, and organizing sensory information.
Stress disorder	A significant emotional disturbance caused by stresses outside the range of normal human

Go to **Cram101.com** for the Practice Tests for this Chapter.

experience is referred to as stress disorder.

Physiology	The study of the functions and activities of living cells, tissues, and organs and of the physical and chemical phenomena involved is referred to as physiology.
Adrenaline	Adrenaline refers to a hormone produced by the adrenal medulla that stimulates sympathetic ANS activity and generally arouses people and heightens their emotional responsiveness.
Longitudinal study	Longitudinal study is a type of developmental study in which the same group of participants is followed and measured for an extended period of time, often years.
Social support	Social Support is the physical and emotional comfort given by family, friends, co-workers and others. Research has identified three main types of social support: emotional, practical, sharing points of view.
Longitudinal design	A research design in which investigators observe one group of subjects repeatedly over a period of time is called a longitudinal design.
Applied psychology	The basic premise of applied psychology is the use of psychological principles and theories to overcome practical problems.
Organizational commitment	Organizational commitment is the extent of an individual's commitment to an organization. There are three major types of commitment, according to Meyer and Allen's three-component model: Affective Commitment; Continuance Commitment; and Normative Commitment.
Noradrenaline	Noradrenaline is released from the adrenal glands as a hormone into the blood, but it is also a neurotransmitter in the nervous system. As a stress hormone, it affects parts of the human brain where attention and impulsivity are controlled. Along with epinephrine, this compound effects the fight-or-flight response, activating the sympathetic nervous system to directly increase heart rate, release energy from fat, and increase muscle readiness.
Cortisol	Cortisol is a corticosteroid hormone that is involved in the response to stress; it increases blood pressure and blood sugar levels and suppresses the immune system. Synthetic cortisol, also known as hydrocortisone, is used as a drug mainly to fight allergies and inflammation.
Catecholamines	Catecholamines are chemical compounds derived from the amino acid tyrosine that act as hormones or neurotransmitters. High catecholamine levels in blood are associated with stress.
Adaptation	Adaptation is a lowering of sensitivity to a stimulus following prolonged exposure to that stimulus. Behavioral adaptations are special ways a particular organism behaves to survive in its natural habitat.
Self-efficacy	Self-efficacy is the belief that one has the capabilities to execute the courses of actions required to manage prospective situations.
Personality	Personality refers to the pattern of enduring characteristics that differentiates a person, the patterns of behaviors that make each individual unique.
Neuroticism	Eysenck's use of the term neuroticism (or Emotional Stability) was proposed as the dimension describing individual differences in the predisposition towards neurotic disorder.
Negative affectivity	Negative affectivity is a personality variable that refers to a tendency to experience negative emotions across many different situations.
Industrial and organizational psychology	Industrial and organizational psychology is the study of the behavior of people in the workplace. Industrial and organizational psychology attempts to apply psychological results and methods to aid workers and organizations.
Incentive	An incentive is what is expected once a behavior is performed. An incentive acts as a reinforcer.
Human factors	Human factors refers to the study of the interaction of people and machines. It is a

technology that applies knowledge of human behavior, cognition, physical capabilities and dimensions to the design of products, equipment, or large-scale systems that can be used easily, effectively and safely by human operators.

Ergonomics	Ergonomics refers to the branch of psychology concerned with the interaction of people and technology; also called engineering psychology or human factors.
Token economy	An environmental setting that fosters desired behavior by reinforcing it with tokens that can be exchanged for other reinforcers is called a token economy.
Work motivation	The conditions and processes responsible for the arousal, direction, magnitude, and maintenance of effort one puts forth in one's job is called the work motivation.
Motivation	In psychology, motivation is the driving force (desire) behind all actions of an organism.
Depersonaliz-tion	Depersonalization is the experience of feelings of loss of a sense of reality. A sufferer feels that they have changed and the world has become less real — it is vague, dreamlike, or lacking in significance.
Applied research	Applied research is done to solve specific, practical questions; its primary aim is not to gain knowledge for its own sake. It can be exploratory but often it is descriptive. It is almost always done on the basis of basic research.
Feedback	Feedback refers to information returned to a person about the effects a response has had.

Go to **Cram101.com** for the Practice Tests for this Chapter.

Cohesiveness	Cohesiveness with respect to conformity is the degree of attraction felt by an individual toward an influencing group.
Process loss	Time spent by group members that is not devoted to task accomplishment is called process loss.
Attention	Attention is the cognitive process of selectively concentrating on one thing while ignoring other things. Psychologists have labeled three types of attention: sustained attention, selective attention, and divided attention.
Norms	In testing, standards of test performance that permit the comparison of one person's score on the test to the scores of others who have taken the same test are referred to as norms.
Group cohesiveness	The strength of the liking relationships linking group members to each other and to the group itself is referred to as group cohesiveness.
Conformity	Conformity is the degree to which members of a group will change their behavior, views and attitudes to fit the views of the group. The group can influence members via unconscious processes or via overt social pressure on individuals.
Piece-rate system	A system that pays employees for each unit of productivity is called a piece-rate system.
Incentive	An incentive is what is expected once a behavior is performed. An incentive acts as a reinforcer.
Motives	Needs or desires that energize and direct behavior toward a goal are motives.
Job satisfaction	A person's attitudes and feelings about his or her job and facets of the job is called job satisfaction.
Organizational commitment	Organizational commitment is the extent of an individual's commitment to an organization. There are three major types of commitment, according to Meyer and Allen's three-component model: Affective Commitment; Continuance Commitment; and Normative Commitment.
Interdependence	Interdependence is a dynamic of being mutually responsible to and dependent on others.
Questionnaire	A self-report method of data collection or clinical assessment method in which the individual being studied checks off items on a printed list, answers multiple-choice questions, or writes out answers to essay questions aimed at producing a selfdescription is called questionnaire.
Construct	A generalized concept, such as anxiety or gravity, is a construct.
Social facilitation	Social facilitation refers to the process by which a person's performance is increased when other members of a group engage in similar behavior.
Social inhibition	Social inhibition is the decline in performance that sometimes occurs when acting in the presence of other people. Research has shown that complex or new tasks are inhibited by the presence of others, whereas performance on simple or well-learned tasks is facilitated.
Additive task	Additive task is when a group's performance is the sum of all the individual members' performances.
Personality	Personality refers to the pattern of enduring characteristics that differentiates a person, the patterns of behaviors that make each individual unique.
Social psychology	Social psychology is the study of the nature and causes of human social behavior, with an emphasis on how people think towards each other and how they relate to each other.
Social loafing	Social loafing is the phenomenon that persons make less effort to achieve a goal when they work in a group than when they work alone. This is one of the main reasons that groups

sometimes perform less than the combined performance of their members working as individuals.

Collectivist	A person who defines the self in terms of relationships to other people and groups and gives priority to group goals is called collectivist.
Affect	A subjective feeling or emotional tone often accompanied by bodily expressions noticeable to others is called affect.
Hypothesis	A specific statement about behavior or mental processes that is testable through research is a hypothesis.
Collectivism	Collectivism is an emphasis on the group, as opposed to the individual. It is syndrome of attitudes and behaviors based on the belief that the basic unit of survival lies within a group, not the individual.
Brainstorming	Brainstorming is an organized approach for producing ideas by letting the mind think without interruption. The term was coined by Alex Osborn.
Shyness	A tendency to avoid others plus uneasiness and strain when socializing is called shyness.
Social anxiety	A feeling of apprehension in the presence of others is social anxiety.
Anxiety	Anxiety is a complex combination of the feeling of fear, apprehension and worry often accompanied by physical sensations such as palpitations, chest pain and/or shortness of breath.
Group polarization	The solidification and further strengthening of a position as a consequence of a group discussion is called a group polarization effect.
Polarization	Polarization is the process of preparing a neuron for firing by creating an internal negative charge in relation to the body fluid outside the cell membrane.
Groupthink	In a groupthink situation, each member of the group attempts to conform his or her opinions to what they believe to be the consensus of the group.
Cognition	The intellectual processes through which information is obtained, transformed, stored, retrieved, and otherwise used is cognition.
Wisdom	Wisdom is the ability to make correct judgments and decisions. It is an intangible quality gained through experience. Whether or not something is wise is determined in a pragmatic sense by its popularity, how long it has been around, and its ability to predict against future events.
Quality circle	A quality circle is a group composed of regular employees who meet together to discuss workplace improvement, and make presentations to management with their ideas.
Motivation	In psychology, motivation is the driving force (desire) behind all actions of an organism.
Industrial/organizational psychology	Industrial/organizational psychology is an applied branch of psychology concerned with behavior of individuals and groups in organizations.

Trait	An enduring personality characteristic that tends to lead to certain behaviors is called a trait. The term trait also means a genetically inherited feature of an organism.
Contingency Theory	The Contingency Theory of Classical Conditioning disagreed on what made a CS a useful predictor. It was more than the number of CS-US pairings, rather, it was the contingency between the CS and US.
Path-goal	In organizational studies, the path-goal model of leadership states that a leader's function is to clear the path toward the goal of the group, by meeting the needs of subordinates. The model was developed jointly by Martin Evans and Robert House.
Sexual harassment	Deliberate or repeated verbal comments, gestures, or physical contact of a sexual nature that is unwanted by the recipient is called sexual harassment.
Groupthink	In a groupthink situation, each member of the group attempts to conform his or her opinions to what they believe to be the consensus of the group.
Feedback	Feedback refers to information returned to a person about the effects a response has had.
Theories	Theories are logically self-consistent models or frameworks describing the behavior of a certain natural or social phenomenon. They are broad explanations and predictions concerning phenomena of interest.
Attitude	An enduring mental representation of a person, place, or thing that evokes an emotional response and related behavior is called attitude.
Expert power	Influence based on the perceived expertise of an individual is referred to as expert power.
Referent power	Referent power is the degree of Influence based on the subordinate's liking for the supervisor.
Coercive power	Coercive power is based on the use of punishments or force.
Job satisfaction	A person's attitudes and feelings about his or her job and facets of the job is called job satisfaction.
Affect	A subjective feeling or emotional tone often accompanied by bodily expressions noticeable to others is called affect.
Punishment	Punishment is the addtion of a stimulus that reduces the frequency of a response, or the removal of a stimulus that results in a reduction of the response.
Discrimination	In Learning theory, discrimination refers the ability to distinguish between a conditioned stimulus and other stimuli. It can be brought about by extensive training or differential reinforcement. In social terms, it is the denial of privileges to a person or a group on the basis of prejudice.
Motives	Needs or desires that energize and direct behavior toward a goal are motives.
Perception	Perception is the process of acquiring, interpreting, selecting, and organizing sensory information.
Threshold	In general, a threshold is a fixed location or value where an abrupt change is observed. In the sensory modalities, it is the minimum amount of stimulus energy necessary to elicit a sensory response.
Leader-member exchange theory	Leader-member exchange theory views leadership from the perspective of individual leader-subordinate pairs.
Exchange theory	A relationship in which the participants expect and desire strict reciprocity in their interactions is referred to as exchange theory.
Motivation	In psychology, motivation is the driving force (desire) behind all actions of an organism.

Go to **Cram101.com** for the Practice Tests for this Chapter.

Go to **Cram101.com** for the Practice Tests for this Chapter.
And, **NEVER** highlight a book again!

Personality	Personality refers to the pattern of enduring characteristics that differentiates a person, the patterns of behaviors that make each individual unique.
Physical attractiveness	Physical attractiveness is the perception of an individual as physically beautiful by other people.
Meta-analysis	In statistics, a meta-analysis combines the results of several studies that address a set of related research hypotheses.
Questionnaire	A self-report method of data collection or clinical assessment method in which the individual being studied checks off items on a printed list, answers multiple-choice questions, or writes out answers to essay questions aimed at producing a selfdescription is called questionnaire.
Factor analysis	Factor analysis is a statistical technique that originated in psychometrics. The objective is to explain the most of the variability among a number of observable random variables in terms of a smaller number of unobservable random variables called factors.
Initiating structure	Initiating structure is a leadership style that is characterized by a concern with task accomplishment.
Stereotype	A stereotype is considered to be a group concept, held by one social group about another.They are often used in a negative or prejudicial sense and are frequently used to justify certain discriminatory behaviors. This allows powerful social groups to legitimize and protect their dominant position
Cross-sectional research	A research method in which people of different ages are compared at the same point in time is called cross-sectional research.
Research design	A research design tests a hypothesis. The basic typess are: descriptive, correlational, and experimental.
Survey	A method of scientific investigation in which a large sample of people answer questions about their attitudes or behavior is referred to as a survey.
Correlation	A statistical technique for determining the degree of association between two or more variables is referred to as correlation.
Semantic differential	Semantic differential is a type of a rating scale designed to measure connotative meaning of objects, events, and concepts. A factor analysis of adjectives typically returns three factors: evaluation, potency, and activity.
Variable	A variable refers to a measurable factor, characteristic, or attribute of an individual or a system.
Social psychology	Social psychology is the study of the nature and causes of human social behavior, with an emphasis on how people think towards each other and how they relate to each other.
Validity	The extent to which a test measures what it is intended to measure is called validity.
Expectancy theory	According to the expectancy theory the amount of effort people exert on a specific task depends on their expectations of the outcome.
Locus of control	The place to which an individual attributes control over the receiving of reinforcers -either inside or outside the self is referred to as locus of control.
Self-efficacy	Self-efficacy is the belief that one has the capabilities to execute the courses of actions required to manage prospective situations.
Anxiety	Anxiety is a complex combination of the feeling of fear, apprehension and worry often accompanied by physical sensations such as palpitations, chest pain and/or shortness of breath.

Self-esteem	Self-esteem refers to a person's subjective appraisal of himself or herself as intrinsically positive or negative to some degree.
Attention	Attention is the cognitive process of selectively concentrating on one thing while ignoring other things. Psychologists have labeled three types of attention: sustained attention, selective attention, and divided attention.
Hypothesis	A specific statement about behavior or mental processes that is testable through research is a hypothesis.
Applied psychology	The basic premise of applied psychology is the use of psychological principles and theories to overcome practical problems.
Hired hands	Hired hands in leader-member exchange theory, are the individuals who are not favored by the supervisor.
Field experiment	A field experiment applies the scientific method to experimentally examine an intervention in the real world rather than in the laboratory. Field experiments generally randomize subjects into treatment and control groups and compare outcomes between these groups.
Control group	A group that does not receive the treatment effect in an experiment is referred to as the control group or sometimes as the comparison group.
Organizational citizenship behavior	Organizational Citizenship Behavior is a special type of work behavior that are defined as individual behaviors that are beneficial to the organization and are discretionary, not directly or explicitly recognized by the formal reward system.
Organizational commitment	Organizational commitment is the extent of an individual's commitment to an organization. There are three major types of commitment, according to Meyer and Allen's three-component model: Affective Commitment; Continuance Commitment; and Normative Commitment.
Equity theory	Equity theory suggests that people are most satisfied with a relationship when the ratio between benefits and contributions is similar.
Stages	Stages represent relatively discrete periods of time in which functioning is qualitatively different from functioning at other periods.
Compensation	In personaility, compensation, according to Adler, is an effort to overcome imagined or real inferiorities by developing one's abilities.
Glass ceiling	A glass ceiling is an unofficial barrier to an upper management or other prominent position within a company or other organization which certain groups are perceived to be unable to cross, due to discrimination.
Gender difference	A gender difference is a disparity between genders involving quality or quantity. Though some gender differences are controversial, they are not to be confused with sexist stereotypes.
Autonomy	Autonomy is the condition of something that does not depend on anything else.
Learning	Learning is a relatively permanent change in behavior that results from experience. Thus, to attribute a behavioral change to learning, the change must be relatively permanent and must result from experience.

Theories	Theories are logically self-consistent models or frameworks describing the behavior of a certain natural or social phenomenon. They are broad explanations and predictions concerning phenomena of interest.
Affect	A subjective feeling or emotional tone often accompanied by bodily expressions noticeable to others is called affect.
Learning	Learning is a relatively permanent change in behavior that results from experience. Thus, to attribute a behavioral change to learning, the change must be relatively permanent and must result from experience.
Anxiety	Anxiety is a complex combination of the feeling of fear, apprehension and worry often accompanied by physical sensations such as palpitations, chest pain and/or shortness of breath.
Perception	Perception is the process of acquiring, interpreting, selecting, and organizing sensory information.
Self-esteem	Self-esteem refers to a person's subjective appraisal of himself or herself as intrinsically positive or negative to some degree.
Questionnaire	A self-report method of data collection or clinical assessment method in which the individual being studied checks off items on a printed list, answers multiple-choice questions, or writes out answers to essay questions aimed at producing a selfdescription is called questionnaire.
Job satisfaction	A person's attitudes and feelings about his or her job and facets of the job is called job satisfaction.
Personality	Personality refers to the pattern of enduring characteristics that differentiates a person, the patterns of behaviors that make each individual unique.
Applied psychology	The basic premise of applied psychology is the use of psychological principles and theories to overcome practical problems.
Management by objectives	Management by Objectives is a process of agreeing upon objectives within an organization so that management and employees buy in to the objectives and understand what they are.
Feedback	Feedback refers to information returned to a person about the effects a response has had.
Survey	A method of scientific investigation in which a large sample of people answer questions about their attitudes or behavior is referred to as a survey.
Meta-analysis	In statistics, a meta-analysis combines the results of several studies that address a set of related research hypotheses.
Attitude	An enduring mental representation of a person, place, or thing that evokes an emotional response and related behavior is called attitude.
Stages	Stages represent relatively discrete periods of time in which functioning is qualitatively different from functioning at other periods.
Variable	A variable refers to a measurable factor, characteristic, or attribute of an individual or a system.
Longitudinal study	Longitudinal study is a type of developmental study in which the same group of participants is followed and measured for an extended period of time, often years.
Psychotherapy	Psychotherapy is a set of techniques based on psychological principles intended to improve mental health, emotional or behavioral issues.
Modeling	A type of behavior learned through observation of others demonstrating the same behavior is

modeling.

Control group	A group that does not receive the treatment effect in an experiment is referred to as the control group or sometimes as the comparison group.
Hawthorne effect	The Hawthorne effect refers to improvements in productivity or quality which result not so much because of intended changes to working conditions, but mainly because the workers are aware of extra attention being paid to them.
Attention	Attention is the cognitive process of selectively concentrating on one thing while ignoring other things. Psychologists have labeled three types of attention: sustained attention, selective attention, and divided attention.
Self-fulfilling prophecy	A self-fulfilling prophecy is a prediction that, in being made, actually causes itself to become true.
Autonomy	Autonomy is the condition of something that does not depend on anything else.
Homeostasis	Homeostasis is the property of an open system, especially living organisms, to regulate its internal environment so as to maintain a stable condition, by means of multiple dynamic equilibrium adjustments controlled by interrelated regulation mechanisms.
Joint optimization	The concept from sociotechnical systems theory that the social system and technical system of an organization must be designed to complement one another is called joint optimization.
Human factors	Human factors refers to the study of the interaction of people and machines. It is a technology that applies knowledge of human behavior, cognition, physical capabilities and dimensions to the design of products, equipment, or large-scale systems that can be used easily, effectively and safely by human operators.
Variance	The degree to which scores differ among individuals in a distribution of scores is the variance.
Motivation	In psychology, motivation is the driving force (desire) behind all actions of an organism.
Self-efficacy	Self-efficacy is the belief that one has the capabilities to execute the courses of actions required to manage prospective situations.
Incentive	An incentive is what is expected once a behavior is performed. An incentive acts as a reinforcer.
Field study	Field study refers to any scientific research study in which data are collected in a setting other than the laboratory.
Reflection	Reflection is the process of rephrasing or repeating thoughts and feelings expressed, making the person more aware of what they are saying or thinking.
Empirical	Empirical means the use of working hypotheses which are capable of being disproved using observation or experiment.
Social support	Social Support is the physical and emotional comfort given by family, friends, co-workers and others. Research has identified three main types of social support: emotional, practical, sharing points of view.
Work-family conflict	A form of role conflict in which family demands and work demands are at odds is the work-family conflict.
Life satisfaction	A person's attitudes about his or her overall life are referred to as life satisfaction.
Social psychology	Social psychology is the study of the nature and causes of human social behavior, with an emphasis on how people think towards each other and how they relate to each other.

Groupthink	In a groupthink situation, each member of the group attempts to conform his or her opinions to what they believe to be the consensus of the group.
Occupational health psychology	An interdisciplinary subfield of psychology concerned with employee health, safety, and well-being is occupational health psychology.
Health psychology	The field of psychology that studies the relationships between psychological factors and the prevention and treatment of physical illness is called health psychology.
Socialization	Social rules and social relations are created, communicated, and changed in verbal and nonverbal ways creating social complexity useful in identifying outsiders and intelligent breeding partners. The process of learning these skills is called socialization.
Negative affectivity	Negative affectivity is a personality variable that refers to a tendency to experience negative emotions across many different situations.
Validity	The extent to which a test measures what it is intended to measure is called validity.
Antecedents	In behavior modification, events that typically precede the target response are called antecedents.
Mentoring	Mentoring refers to a developmental relationship between a more experienced individual and a less experienced partner sometimes referred to as a protégé. In well-designed formal mentoring programs, there are program goals, schedules, and training.
Trait	An enduring personality characteristic that tends to lead to certain behaviors is called a trait. The term trait also means a genetically inherited feature of an organism.
Reciprocity	Reciprocity, in interpersonal attraction, is the tendency to return feelings and attitudes that are expressed about us.
Transfer of training	The concept of transfer of training states that knowledge or abilities acquired in one area aids the acquisition of knowledge or abilities in other areas. When prior learning is helpful, it is called positive transfer. When prior learning inhibits new learning, it is called negative transfer.

Go to **Cram101.com** for the Practice Tests for this Chapter.

Printed in the United States
144314LV00001B/27/A